Death of Democracy: The Erosion of Freedom

Doctrine of the Second American Revolution

By J.C. "Jake" Laughton

This book is dedicated with love to my entire

family and to the few I am fortunate enough to

call My Friends.

Table of Contents

Chapter 1

A Renewed Purpose: The Erosion of Freedom

John Kennedy once said, "Let us be the masters, not the victims of our history".

Current US Senator and Presidential Candidate and former First Lady Hillary Clinton was quoted as saying, "We're all in it together".

President Bush calls America the "Ownership Society". Not only does he believe it but he supports it with his Policies.

To paraphrase a commonly used expression in America, 1% of the population of the US owns and controls 85% of it.

Recently I watched George Carlin doing a comedy stand up show on HBO; in one bit from his show he called the People that run the US "The Owners of America".

In the Michael Moore movie "Sicko", Americans who now live in France tell us the Government there is concerned enough about its people to enact laws that not only protect them but give them extra things to make their lives easier. Some of the things mentioned include full health care, but 5 weeks of PAID vacation each year. 5 weeks of paid vacation each year makes them nicely rested and refreshed and as a result France has one of the world's highest productivity rates from its workers.

When asked why the French government gave them all these great perks, the answer was straight forward and to the point, "Here the government is afraid of the People, in American the People are afraid of their government". Most important here is the fact that over 90% of the French people vote. Voting is the power that the people have in a democracy.

In America people are afraid that if they stand up to the government that the government will take away its freedom, but this is already happening. In the pages that follow I show you how this is happening and the key factors that point directly to it. We as a nation are being lead towards a time and place in history where democracy no longer exists. In fact Democracy is all but gone already. Democracy was established here in America to fight the financial oppression of England's King George, not only taxation without any representation, but price fixing and the elimination of open competition that allowed the British to charge whatever price it wanted for its goods.

Democracy is where the people elect others to enact laws, rules and regulations that serve their collective conscious for the common good of all. Nowadays, corporations pay lawmakers, through huge campaign donations and fabulously extravagant FREE vacations and trips, to enact laws, rules and regulations for the good of the Corporations ONLY, with no regard to the People who are supposed to have that sole privilege.

If 1% of the US population owns so much of it, what exactly does that mean? For you and me in the 99% group, what it means is this; there are 3 million people worth at least $1 million that is exactly 1%. So in the US there are 297 million people who do not have a million dollars or are not worth one million dollars. There is a shift in what defines the middle class, people like me who a few years ago would have been considered middle class can no longer say that. Anyone who does not yet have a worth of one million, but has income of more than $250,000.00 per year can be labeled as middle class. To truly be "middle class" you either have to have an income that will earn you a million in less than 5 years or be in the class of millionaires who have a worth of fewer than 2 million dollars. Those who are worth more than 3 million dollars are not the upper class, but the "super class". And those of the 297 million Americans who are not worth a million dollars are the "sub class".

Back about 20 years ago give or take a few years, there was a commercial on TV with a man saying, " I make more money than my father made during his life but I have so much less and can't afford to give my family all the things that my dad did". The commercial was about starting an account to save for your retirement, given the statement made by the man in the commercial, how could he or anyone save for their retirement? One of my favorite retirement benefits (and I am being sarcastic here) is the 401K that companies use to lure minimum wages employees. How is a single person that can't afford even the rent for an apartment, going to be able to contribute to a 401K plan?

In the last 30 years every price in America has risen nearly 1000% with some prices going higher then that. Our government leaders are knowingly creating a situation where a dictatorship may quickly come to be. President Bush has suggested that he would like to be dictator of America.

The term doctrine is used to refer to a principle of law, in the common law traditions, established through a history of past decisions, such as the doctrine of self-defense, or the principle of fair use.

My message is delivered in what I call the 'Erosion of Freedom' doctrine made up of 4 factors they are,

1. Freedom is taken away by stifling and controlling your money, this control over your finances is being accomplished with high prices on everything you buy.

2. Elections are being manipulated to get puppet candidates in office; the greatest example of this is the Election of George Bush.

3. Creating and maintaining a climate of fear is central to this discussion. Creating fear also has a side detriment in that it quite often creates Panic Buying.

4. The government is actively involved in creating higher prices in the Meat, Diary and Produce industries.

In the pages that follow you will read examples of this taking place now. I use personal information, facts and opinions to illustrate to you what I am describing and how you can start doing something to change this downward spiral and restore true freedom for you, your family and your descendants for generations to come.

The first super hero ever created was Superman and his Credo was "To Fight for Truth, Justice and The American Way". In the 2006 remake "Superman Returns" Superman's credo is now Truth, Justice and that other stuff! So why was "and The American Way" dropped? To be less objectionable to an international audience? Are they saying that the OLD "American Way" is dead and gone?

This book is not just about the current President George Bush, but since it was written while he is in office he gets lots of the blame for the problems in the US today. George Bush is just one shining example of the poor leadership that has lead us to this point in American history.

There are horrible things going on in this country, I feel that if Americans don't act now, these trends will continue regardless of who is our president. Democracy, our democracy has been swept away. In my 47 years, I have often heard the phrase used in regards to a Dictator in a foreign land, "That absolute power corrupts absolutely" President Bush has been caught on tape saying, "I wish this was a dictatorship, it would be easier to handle". Usually a dictator is at least a smart person, but Bush is out there in LALA land, a 1-dimensional product of wealth and privilege.

Chapter 2
Recent Evidence

Recently I came across a new book by noted Best Selling author Naomi Wolf.

The End of America: A Letter of Warning to a Young Patriot by Naomi Wolf

Book Description from Amazon.com

Wolf explains how events of the last six years parallel steps taken in the early years of the 20th century's worst dictatorships such as Germany, Russia, China and Chile. Recent history has profound lessons for us in the U.S. today about how fascist, totalitarian, and other repressive leaders seize and maintain power, especially in what were once democracies. The secret is that these leaders all tend to take very similar, parallel steps.

The Founders of this nation were so deeply familiar with tyranny and the habits and practices of tyrants that they set up our checks and balances precisely out of fear of what is unfolding today. We are seeing these same kinds of tactics now closing down freedoms in America.

Reviews for the End of America: A Letter of Warning to a Young Patriot by Naomi Wolf

"You will be shocked and disturbed by this book. Most Americans reject outright any comparison of post 9/11 America with the fascism and totalitarianism of Nazi Germany or Pinochet's Chile. Sadly, the parallels and similarities, what Wolf calls the 'echoes' between those societies and America today, are all too compelling."
—Michael Ratner, Center for Constitutional Rights

"Naomi Wolf sounds the alarm for all American patriots. We must come together as a nation and

recommit ourselves to the fundamental American idea that no president, whether Democrat or Republican, will ever be given unchecked power."
—WesBoyd, co-founder, MoveOn.org

"The framers of our Constitution fully understood that it can happen here. Patriots like Madison, Paine, and Franklin would certainly applaud Naomi Wolf and recognize her as a sister in their struggle."
—Mark Crispin Miller, author of Fooled Again

"Naomi Wolf's End of America is a vivid, urgent, mandatory wake-up call that addresses momentous issues of tyranny, democracy, and survival."
—Blanche Wiesen Cook, author of the three-volume Eleanor Roosevelt

The first factor in the Erosion of Freedom is to stifle and control you by controlling your money.

This book and many like it represent a new trend in America; people are beginning to think and feel that the American Government is out of control, this is not a mere guess but a FACT.

Chapter 3
Background and History

Michael Moore has made 2 movies about recent issues in America, Fahrenheit 911 and Sicko. I want to start by addressing the issues in Fahrenheit 911 and later I will talk about Sicko. Both of Michael Moore's observations are pivotal, yet like many he does not go far enough, you can only do and say so much in a movie, not all of the issues are covered and the solutions that would help us resolve them are not clearly and accurately stated.

Michael Moore has started the change in thinking, but for it to truly work, it must be laid completely open and the solutions clearly defined for all to see and act upon. I strive to awaken every men and women in America to take action. Every person who calls themselves an American, must understand what is really going on and MUST work with their follow Americans to make things right.

Every American that has complained about higher gas prices, higher grocery prices, higher medical expenses, higher utilities, higher housing prices, higher car prices, higher auto repair bills, or higher insurance prices has an interest and an obligation to do something about it. You may think at times that you are at the mercy of unknown forces or unforeseen factors; I will show you and explain to you exactly who and what they are.

All I ask is that you read what I have written here and then decide your course of action. I will present facts and opinions and conclusions, many of the facts that I do present are based on personal observations. I lay out the salary from my actual job and the taxes and expenditures that eat it up every month. I use my own Electric bill as an example. One thing must be clear before we start and that is that you have cause to think about your own life and family and apply what I say to your own experiences and make a decision to act in some way. Thinking about change is a good start but you must take action and you must bind yourself with others in taking an action to affect change. Only as a large group can Americans make changes. Change must take place, so read on and keep an open mind.

With that in mind let's start with a brief history of how democracy started in America.

The Boston Tea Party was an act of protest by the American colonists against Great Britain in which they destroyed many crates of tea bricks on ships in Boston Harbor. This incident is cited as the turning point that helped to spark the American Revolution.

On Thursday, December 16, 1773, the evening before the tea was due to be landed, the

Sons of Liberty thinly disguised as Mohawk Indians, left the massive protest meeting and headed toward Griffin's Wharf, where lay the ships The Dartmouth and the newly arrived Beaver and Eleanor. Swiftly and efficiently, casks of tea were brought up from the hold to the deck; this was reasonable proof that some of the "Indians" were, in fact, longshoremen. The casks were opened and the tea dumped overboard; the work, lasting well into the night, was quick, thorough, and efficient. By dawn, 90,000 lbs (45 tons) of tea worth an estimated £10,000 had been consigned to the waters of Boston Harbor. Nothing else had been damaged or stolen, except a single padlock accidentally broken and anonymously replaced not long thereafter. Tea washed up on the shores around Boston for weeks.

The Stamp Act of 1765 and the Townshend Acts of 1767 angered colonists regarding British decisions on taxing the colonies despite a lack of representation in the Parliament in England.

Shipping Merchant John Hancock, (Yes this is the same man who chaired the committee in the approval of and was the First Signer of the Declaration of Independence), organized a boycott of tea from China sold by the British East India Company, whose sales in the colonies then fell from 320,000 pounds (145,000 kg) to 520 pounds (240 kg). By 1773, the company had large debts, huge stocks of tea in its warehouses and no prospect of selling it. The British government passed the Tea Act, which allowed the East India Company (a British Importing Company) to sell tea to the colonies directly and without "payment of any customs or duties whatsoever" in Britain, instead paying the much lower American duty. This tax break allowed the East India Company to sell for lower prices than those offered by the colonial merchants and smugglers. (In other words the British government manipulated both the tax laws and the prices in its own favor).

Excerpts from Wikipedia.

The whole purpose of the American Revolution was to break free from England's control over everything financial. The Declaration of Independence lists in several places the specific abuses of high pricing controls by the King of England onto the colonies. I use the above example of the Boston Tea Party to show how England used every means it had to not only tax us as much as it could but force the setting of higher prices that the colonials had to pay.

The people of the United States of America no longer control their lives or their money. US Corporations control everything now. Rather than tax you directly the government is manipulated into allowing prices to be controlled by Corporations who set prices and reap higher and higher profits each year. The trade off for the US government is that by allowing prices to rise at the will of the Corporations, instead of taxing you more, they collect those additional tax dollars from the profits of the corporations. This tactic makes it appear that the problem is economic when it is not.

In other words the Corporations raise prices, and you pay more, but you are not taxed more. The corporations pay the same taxes, the same percentages, not the same amounts, so the Corporations pay higher amounts of taxes but still at the same percentages as they did 10 years ago. All the while making huge profits.

Here is an example of this, in the past Company A had sales of $10 million per year and paid 10% in taxes or $1 million. Now Company A has raised its prices 5 times and now makes $50 million yet still sells the same number of units it sold before. So they have $50 million in yearly income but they still pay 10% in taxes or $5 million. Instead of having $9 million in profits they now have $45 million in profit.

This is a static example to illustrate what is happening in our country. On previous pages I mentioned higher gas Prices, grocery bills, car prices, housing, utilities etc. I will give exact examples of all of these in subsequent pages, But for now I think you can start to see my point.

Most people would quickly come to the conclusion that the tragedies of 9\11 are where it starts, but it actually starts much earlier than that.

For the moment we will discuss the Bush Administration.

Michael Moore's Fahrenheit 911 shows that the Bush Family was actively involved, with other US corporations, a group I have dubbed the Iraq Club, in finding a way into the vast fortunes of the oil wealth in Iraq, and well before the elections of 2000. The Bush Family furnished the candidate and the whole group put a plan together.

With its plans to manipulate an election, if necessary, this group of US corporations, the Iraq Club set out to place their puppet candidate into the Presidency.

At this point I think I should qualify why this man is nothing more than a puppet. He comes from a very wealthy and powerful family of Texas Oil Millionaires, or probably

Billionaires. Both oil start ups that his family gave him, he ran into the ground, wasting millions of dollars. The only going business that he had his hands in was also bought for him by his family, that of lead owner of a Texas Baseball Team. As owner of the baseball team he was a figure head only and had no real duties, hence he could not run the baseball franchise into the ground. This very average man was pushed and poised and groomed to become President. As a public official this man cannot keep his mouth shut, insulting African Americans and wishing his presidency was a dictatorship. These are the clear signs of a man of average intelligence behaving like the spoiled rich brat that he is.

Things were set into place and the election proceeded seemingly without issue, this is the great deception however, as the fix was already well in place months before the election.

The night of the presidential election, although close, showed that Vice President Al Gore had won the Popular Vote and the Electoral College vote, to become the next President. By awarding Florida to Al Gore, this gave him the Presidency. Florida has always gone to the Democratic Candidate; this was the status quo, if you will.

By awarding Al Gore Florida, before all the votes had actually been counted, was where the fix kicked in. Bush campaign officials protested, while the election was still going on, saying their information shows Bush taking Florida. HOW would they know this so early on election night, unless they knew for certain that the results could be changed to show their candidate had won? In an election that would be close Florida was key in making this fix work, it was the only state big enough to effect the election outcome.

George Bush's younger brother was the Governor of Florida, a person born and raised in Texas, was the governor of Florida? Florida's chief election official was placed in that position by Governor Jeb Bush, and was a long time family friend of the Bushes. This person had also had numerous financial ventures with the Bush Family.

Thousands of ballots in Florida could not be counted due to the voting machines leaving bits of the ballot paper hanging from the back of the ballots, what was referred to as chafe. It seems the correct thing to do would be to hand clean these ballots, removing the bits of paper. Instead these ballots were ruled by that Florida election official as invalid. It would not be until after the vote was certified by Congress and

George Bush was safely in the White House, that strangely enough, these supposedly invalid ballots showed a majority win in Florida for Al Gore.

The votes in Florida were close, so by invalidating a certain number of ballots they were able to shift the results of the election in favor of their candidate, the Governor's brother. Since these ballots were recorded as invalid and never counted, regardless of what they proved or didn't prove, they would not be allowable or admissible as court evidence, EVER!

The constitution says that the Congress must ratify or certify the election. This was debated in Congress for many weeks. It was a brave man in Al Gore that stood and followed the Constitution to the letter in these proceedings. House Representative after Representative stood up to question the election, but much to his credit, Al Gore's great character guided him in doing the right thing. As the Vice President it was Al Gore's primary job to preside over the Senate, but without the ability to raise an objection. Every time a Representative made an objection to the election, Al Gore repeated that it must be a Senator to make a formal objection, not One Senator ever stood up to object. Why? Did they all feel that this was fair and just? I find it so difficult to believe that not one senator objected, I am very sure that several did, but not one had the character, the guts or the backbone to stand up and say so, this was a terrible shame to America.

Added note: On October 12, 2007, Former Vice President Al Gore won the Nobel Peace Prize for his Academy Award winning film, "An Inconvenient Truth" The film is a documentary on Global Warming. I will save my thoughts on Global Warming for my next book.

Since so many Representatives questioned the election results and not one Senator did, I would have to believe that the fix had been set here as well, just in case, either through coercion or bribery. More probably, and just as believable is that maybe these Senators already knew that an objection was pointless, because all those "invalid ballots" could not be used in court to change the rigged election results. Hence why raise an objection to the election, that when all was said and done would not have put Al Gore in the White House. Where was the collective conscious of the Senate to uphold the truth?

This is the second factor in the Erosion of Freedom.

Chapter 4
The Bush Legacy of Lies

8 Months into Bush's Presidency, 2 jet planes slammed into the World Trade Center Towers, 1 plane hit the Pentagon and a fourth crashed into the ground in Pennsylvania. It was later revealed that the fourth plane was supposed to crash into the White House. If you wanted to hurt the US badly, you target the Capitol Building, not just the White House. It is well known that the President was sitting in a classroom in Florida, of all places, when the President's Chief of Staff whispered in his ear that the US was under attack. We all know the president did nothing but sit there.

(From "Fahrenheit 911")

I definitely cannot understand why the knot head just sat there. I have heard rumblings about a conspiracy, but the thing with conspiracy theory is that there is never any hard evidence. Many innocent people were killed in the World Trade Center towers and the Pentagon, and many people are still suffering from that faithful day, but otherwise the government itself wasn't really hurt. As I stated above the two best targets would have been the Capitol Building and the White House. Two jet planes into the Capitol Building and one into the White House during business hours would have really crippled the US.

Even if they missed the President as they would have done that day, the Vice President who presides over the Senate and the Speaker of the House most likely would have been killed along with most of the Senators and House Members. The Vice President replaces the President as second in line if the President dies or is killed, and the Speaker of the House is 3rd in line. In fact many of those in line to the presidency would have been killed.

Crashing into the World Trade Center, made a statement against the vast wealth of the

US, but not a political one. What was supposed to happen was a financial meltdown of global proportions. The financial meltdown never happened. Crashing planes into the Pentagon served no political point either. The people killed in the World Trade Center and the Pentagon crashes were tragic, they were innocent victims, no political person was killed. Crashing a plane into the White House when the president was in Florida, was absolutely pointless, it only showed that these buildings are subject to an attack. I find it difficult to think that Al-Qaida thought that they had won any kind of victory at all. The death of thousands of innocent lives does one thing and one thing only they fuel the fires of revenge.

Many people have asked me why destroy the World Trade Center, why hurt us financially? Why create a global financial meltdown? Here is the truth, it may shock you, you may hate me for saying it, but curious enough, is has to do with Jewish People.

The US supports and maintains a strong relationship with Israel. The Muslims and most of the Arab World don't like being forced to have a Jewish Nation in their midst. And if you recall in the first Persian Gulf War Saddam Hussein fired scud missiles into Israel. Our support of Israel is a guilt reflex reaction to what Hitler did to the Jews in the Second World War.

All during the war the US, and most of the world had no idea that the Holocaust was going on. After the war was over we saw what had happened to these people and guilt sat in. We had dragged our feet for several years while war raged in Europe, in fact it was not until the Japanese bombed Pearl Harbor in Hawaii, that we jumped into the war at all. So after 4 long years of bombing Germany and planning to enter the war in Europe we put together a force to invade France.

By the time the war was over some 6 million European Jews had been put to death. Because the US had not moved quicker and would have thereby ended the war years sooner, millions of those put to death might have survived. Guilt set in. We vowed from that day forward to support and defend the creation of a Jewish nation.

Michael Scheur, the former head of the CIA's Bin Laden Unit and author of the book 'Marching Toward Hell', has stated that "In defense of Israel, the US should not spend one more dollar or risk one more American life!"

Now the Iraq Club had its reason for the US to invade Iraq. The President assured us that Iraq had taken part in the plane crashes and had weapons of Mass Destruction, oh yeah and a shit load of oil in the ground for the taking, they didn't say!

In the First Persian Gulf War, Desert Storm, Iraq had clearly invaded and took over its neighboring sovereign country of Kuwait; we went in and chased them out and all of this with the full approval of the UN.

This time however Bush and the Iraq Club never got UN approval, but did that stop them? Nope. The US and the British invaded Iraq. Some 4 or 5 years ago the President claimed that it was all over, yet we are still there. Scandal after scandal comes out of Iraq everyday.

Blackwater; a private US security force that pays former US soldiers $1000.00 a day to fight as mercenary soldiers is in Iraq. A private security force garrisoning a country? (Added note, Blackwater has since been pulled out of Iraq for opening fire on innocent people, among other crimes).

180,000 US civilian-contractors are in the country as I write this. They are there to rebuild. The big scandal is that all these contractors are there with million dollar contracts in hand; many have been paid in full yet haven't built a thing. One of these companies gets $10 million to provide air traffic control and security at the Baghdad Airport, yet no planes land or have ever taken off from there since we invaded the country and seized the airport some 5 years ago. There is one scandalous story after another of these kinds of illegal, unethical and immoral dealings coming out of Iraq. Let's hear it for

Democracy and our way of life! The military troops and the Blackwater soldiers are there as an occupying force.

For more details on Blackwater and all the scandals read Pigs at the Trough by Arianna Huffington.

Today's News bit on Yahoo.com October 3, 2007

US congress gives $150 billion for the war.

The same congress that said the war was wrong!

Today's News bit on Yahoo.com October 4, 2007

House of Representatives move on a bill to push troop withdrawals.

I just have one more question before I move forward and that concerns the World Trade Center.

Chapter 5

The World Trade Center of Fear

Why is it still just a deep, empty hole in the ground 6 years later?

Nothing would tell those who crashed planes into the towers to go to HELL better and faster than to rebuild the towers. As long as we don't move to rebuild them we show them we are Afraid! There have been stories about this design or that one, police restrictions, police restrictions? Since when does the NYPD tell the People of the US what to do? Critics will say it is more complicated then this, but it is not. There is a committee of officials and private sectors consultants that was put together to rebuild the Towers, they are making salaries in excess of $200,000.00, BUT Nothing is being Built.

I will say for the record that I do not like Donald Trump, he walks the streets like a self made man, a god among us if you will, someone to be worshiped, which is his ego but in fact he comes from money, lots of Money! He used that money to take it a step further and become a billionaire real estate Mogul.

But "The Donald's" idea to rebuild both World Trade Center Towers was absolutely the right thing to do! For this I will applaud him. Defy them and our own fear by rebuilding the towers!

I trash the billionaires a lot, the reason for this is most of them are not self made. They started with millions made by a now dead relative, exploited the system and are now revered for what they have done. That old saying "it takes money to make money" is really true! We revere them because we want what they have, but what they have should belong to all of us, and by us I mean the 99%, not the 1%. After all, the money that they have was money taken from us by higher prices.

So let's look at all we have talked about so far; a group of US corporations looking to get into Iraq, a fixed election that put a knot head puppet in the White House, a terrorist attack in New York and Washington, an invasion into Iraq fueled with lies and the promise of revenge, daily symbols to remind us to be afraid. Remember the Terror Alert System? Or the Bird flu 'Pandemic' that they seem to revive every week? That which would be our defining act of defiance, spitting in the face of our fears by rebuilding the World Trade Center Towers, has not happened.

The third factor in the Erosion of Freedom is to create fear and panic among the people. (The terror alert system was an attempt to maintain that fear level in the population. Fear Creates 'Panic Buying', recall the Y2K scare they played on us, people lined up around the block to buy bottled water just in case. Or how about the Oil Crisis of 1974)

Chapter 6

Who's Responsible?

You might think that this is where it starts, but it goes all the way back to Nixon, in Michael Moore's movie Sicko; we see that Nixon started the Health Care Plague that we know today as HMOs. In addition to the HMO monster, Nixon did one other thing, to avoid paying huge war debts from the Vietnam War...

In 1971, President Richard Nixon removed the US dollar from the gold standard, ending the predominance of gold in the international monetary system.

The gold standard was a system in which international currencies are tied to a specific amount of gold. The foundation of the gold standard is that a currency's value is supported by some weight in gold. Inherently, it makes sense to value currency by some tangible and precious resource; otherwise, currency is just paper bills.

Nations now valued their currencies by the fiat system instead, i.e. governments took their currencies off the gold standard and simply dictated the value of their money.

From "What is the Gold Standard" by Tarik Abdel-Monem

Since 1971 prices have risen at alarming rates. Look at the price of Gas. In 1971 it was 25-30 cents per gallon, now it's $3.00 and more per gallon. At the end of World War II it was about 10 cents per gallon, so in 25 years it rose 2.5 to 3 times. 10 years ago it was around a $1.50 per gallon. So in 35 years it has risen not 100% that would be double; it has in fact been raised 10 times that 100%, or 1000%. This is not based on inflation or supply and demand economics as most "experts" want you to believe, however if you value the current pricing by inflation alone; since WWII gas would cost about 38 cents per gallon.

The first thing George Bush did upon entering the White House in 2001 was to remove the price cap from refined gas prices. Prior to that time gas had a 17% limit on it. Refineries and retailers could only mark up the price 17% over what it cost them. In the late 70s a barrel of oil cost $35-40, yesterday Oct, 2007 it costs $79. Double the price for a barrel of oil yet we are paying more than quadruple for gas. In '78 gas was around 75 cents a gallon. If you double that, the price is $1.50, using this logic that should be the current price, but we are paying 2 times that price.

You may be saying how does this happen? Well in June the oil companies announced that they had to shut down some refineries for "routine maintenance" Amazingly enough they have been doing this every year for the last 5 years to keep the price up! I had one friend tell me that it makes sense for them to do routine maintenance every year, but I have to ask why do this in the summer months when gas prices are slightly higher normally for vacation and tourist travel and why right before hurricane season?

Then they said in August that because of Hurricanes the prices had to rise, so that we would pay more. The real price of a barrel of oil hardly changed because the hurricane scare didn't happen this year. "Any lie that the public will believe" will keep the oil corporations' profits up and our wallets emptier.

The pricing of a barrel of oil is called a future, or the price of what gas will cost 3 months from now. But have you ever noticed that the price of a barrel of oil 3 months from now will cause the price of gas to rise the very next day! The oil companies state that the reason is that the oil costs them more, in fact it costs far less to buy it today than the price they are referencing in the Futures Market; this is the way they ensure they make the higher profits now, instead of 3 months from now. Look at the financial pages if you can understand all that crap, they are making daily record profits!

The US government states that we have a 4-6 month supply of oil reserves. I want to know why we don't stop buying oil from foreign countries every time the price goes up. We stop buying for 2 weeks and the price would drop like a stone; as soon as the lower price is stable again we buy at the lower rate. Even if we had to do this several times eventually the foreign countries would get the message! But they could counter by lowering their production to help drive the prices back up. Anyway this will never happen, because no matter what price is paid for a barrel of oil, the oil corporations will continue to buy it and sell it at the higher prices for 2 reasons.

1. We will continue to pay for it no matter how high the price
2. Their profit margin stays higher than it would at the lower prices.

So you may be asking at this point how the oil corporations get away with this. In the past, gas prices were set based on the economic principle of supply and demand. A company decided to make 1 year's worth of product, and then a price could be set that would sell those products within 1 year's time. If the product sold better than expected the price went up slightly while the company made more product to have 1 year's worth of inventory once again; this would be a higher amount of product since the product itself was selling better than expected. Once production has brought the inventory up to the new level, production would stop or slow down and the higher price would be lower somewhat, not to the initial price it first sold for, but to something just a percent or 2 higher to account for the higher demand.

Two things happened in the recent past that is significant here because they deal with how all prices are manipulated now in this country.

1. Nixon pulled the US off the Gold Standard,

2. and then in 1974 during the Yom Kippur War, OPEC stopped selling The US oil because we support Israel.

This caused the "gas crisis" and taught us how to panic over gasoline.

You have probably heard this before many times, but I will state it again. Oil Companies and most US corporations are what are known as publicly traded corporations. What that means is that they are listed with the SEC, The Securities and Exchange Commission, to do one thing, raise money and they do this by selling stocks. A stock is ownership equity in a corporation. When you buy a stock, you buy a piece of that company. The SEC has only 2 legal requirements for a publicly traded corporation. Exact, clear and accurate accounting is the first one, remember Enron. The second is it must make its shareholders' money. Must make money!

These corporations' shareholders hire people to run these companies, pay them million dollar salaries all with the sole purpose of making them as much money as possible.

Let me ask you one question.

How many people do you know that actually own stocks?

I went to Mid Town Manhattan and asked 100 people if they knew of anyone who owned stocks in a US Corporation, not one single person could actually state that they knew anyone and I do mean anyone who owned stocks.

So I went to Wall Street, also in Manhattan and asked 100 people the same question. You are going to be as surprised as I was to hear the results of my little poll. Out of 100 people 1 person knew someone who owned stocks, 11 of those I polled knew people, not personally; who were clients of the firms they worked at, who owned stock. Nothing fancy or scientific about this poll, I took a piece of paper, numbered both sides to 100 and asked the question do you know anyone who owns stocks and then I recorded all the yes and the no answers.

Of the results from 200 people, less than ½ of a percent knew anyone that owned stocks. Only 5.5 percent said they knew anyone who owned stocks, yet they all mentioned that they did not know them personally. I can name dozens of people that I do not know personally who own stocks. Everyone knows who the richest man in the world is, Bill Gates, hey he owns stocks! Most responders seemed to understand that I wanted to know if they knew anyone personally, like a relative or friend.

Chapter 7
The Great Communicator

At this point in our story a new player comes forward in the form of Ronald Reagan. I know that my critics will come out of the woodwork on this issue, but it must be said.

Reagan and his decade of "Reaganomics" are crucial to the truth. What Reagan did was to break up large corporations like AT&T. AT& T was a monopoly.

Yes the evilest of all corporations, the monopoly. The idea of the monopoly is that it is pure evil; it locks out competition and choice. The fact that the AT&T Board members were some of the richest people at the time may have something to do with it. Bill Clinton went after Microsoft for being a monopoly, remember? Yet what is funny is that these 2 corporations had better products and at lower costs than their competitors. But the fact is that just like the AT&T board, Bill Gates was unbelievably wealthy. At the time of the Microsoft Monopoly proceedings, Bill Gates was worth more than 100 billion dollars, worse still was that Bill Gates did not give money to Washington law makers, so just like AT&T, Microsoft had to be punished. If you are the super rich and you don't give Washington law makers their share, you will get punished. Remember this is supposed to be a democracy!

Reagan broke up these large corporations through deregulation. Before AT&T was broke apart phone service costs like $3.00 a month for local unlimited service. Toll and long distance charges were additional, but not an arm and a leg to pay for. After the break up, which was to punish the super wealthy few that owned AT&T, things went nuts. I really don't know how to say it better than that, prices soared for phone service and have NEVER come back down. AT&T still owned every phone line in America, but because the deregulation effect was not controlled by law, AT&T got to charge high rates just for the new smaller phone companies to use its phone lines.

What a jump in prices! I don't know anyone with a home phone who doesn't pay $45 to $50 per month for a bundled package of services, you don't need them all, but they won't offer you just phone service, they have it and have to give it to you if you request it but most people don't know that, and what they do more often then not is tell you that one service by itself is no longer available, that lie usually does the trick. At $45 that is an increase of 1500%. Has anyone in the 99% of the population had their salary rise like that in 35 years? Minimum wage has only barely tripled (300%) in that amount of time. From around $2 an hour to just about $6-7 an hour now, it does depend on where you live. How do you keep up with prices that have risen

1000-1500% when you salary has grown less than 300%?

The problem with deregulating laws is that they only tell them what they are not allowed to do, so if it does not say that they have to cap what they charge you, they will do anything that is not prohibited or charge anything that the Market will bare.

It was back at the time of the AT&T Break up that Saturday Night Live did a small bit that looked like a commercial, but in fact was a comedy sketch. It talked about things with the use of your phone, how much it costs, but what was so true then was the closing line of the bit, "We're AT&T, you broke us up and now you have to pay".

Added note: Reaganomics was such a great thing (sarcasm here) that the stock market crashed on October, 1987 its worst day since the Great Depression.

We are being bled dry here, and not just by the Oil and Phone companies.

Chapter 8

A Job Is Just Over Broke

Greed! Greed! Greed!

The Forbes 400 List

This is Forbes Magazine's list of the 400 richest people in America. In 2005 if you were worth $800 Million, you made the list. In 2006 you needed to have at least $950 million. The 2007 List just came out and no one with less than $1.3 billion made it. 400 Americans with a worth of 1.3 Billion or more, this is outrageous! That means that this year there are now billionaires who don't qualify as one of the top 400 richest people.

Notice how quickly the super rich get richer! Higher prices without an economic factor behind them like inflation, creates higher profit margins.

My own salary has not gone up a dime in the last few years and it only did that because I went out and found a higher paying job, but no raises, no bonuses, I don't even get the travel allowance from the company that is stated in writing in the employee hand book. I have obviously done a good enough job to keep it for over 2 years, my customers' love me, but my employer couldn't care less.

Every time I have brought up the travel expense reimbursement, I get the old" well if you aren't happy you can go to work somewhere else." Most people that work in New York City get some sort of travel expense (Which is a tax deduction for any company, including the one I work for) to get to and from work, but because my company is based in California, I get treated this way. Yeah, Yeah, I know, you are sitting there saying 'you should sue and get your travel expense money', but it doesn't work that way, if I file a claim with the Labor board I will get the money, but there is no law that can prevent my employer from firing me the next day. California has a 'Without cause' clause in its employment laws.

The revenue from the Hotels I service is over $180,000 a month, this varies but on average it is $180,000.00 monthly, which is $2,160,000.00; yes $2.1 Million a year! My Salary is $4000.00 monthly or $48,000.00 annually. Sounds good right, but try living in New York on that. I work in Mid town Manhattan were the annual median income is $59,000 per year, but I as a college graduate I get $48,000! Not that I am not very smart or the fact that I am a college graduate but, this is simply due to a California Company that takes advantage of me. They tried 6 or 7 guys for this position before they hired me; none of the others had the technical skills or the ability to work well with 5 Star Hotel employees.

I travel to Midtown Manhattan Monday through Friday. I have to drive to the train station which is 25 miles from my house, that's 3 gallons of gas round trip at $3.00 per gallon, the current price today, for $9.00. Train Station parking fee is $2.00 per day. I buy a roundtrip train ticket which costs 20.50 daily. When I get to Manhattan I have to take the subway once each way, daily. That's $2.00 each way for $4.00. So my daily reimbursable expenses are$35.50, which my employer does not pay. First half of the month there are 10 travel days and the 2nd half of the month there are 11-12 travel days.

My salary is $2000 twice a month. I have a wife and 2 kids, but look at the taxes I have to pay:

Federal Income Tax	39.18
Social Security Tax	124.00
Medicare Tax	29.00
New York State Income Tax	73.43

New York SUI/SDI Tax   1.30

That leaves us $1733.09 after taxes. What gets me is the New York State Income Tax is twice my Federal Tax and Social Security Tax is 3 times my Federal Tax. Out of this I have travel expenses that my employer is supposed to repay me for but doesn't.

So my check after taxes is $1733.09, now let's deduct 10 days of travel or $355.00, which leaves 1378.09. That is the first half of the month.

In the second half of the month, deduct 12 days travel or $426.00, which leaves us $1307.09

So after taxes, instead of having $1733.09 times 2 or $3466.18 monthly, I have $2685.18.

Most people reading this would say that's not so bad for a month, but WAIT, I haven't paid any of the bills yet!

Rent	1100.00
Cable TV	69.95
Internet via Cable Modem	49.95
Vonage phone	31.95
Car Payment for a used car	175.00
Car Insurance	71.00
Electricity	130.00
Electricity during the winter	375.00
College loan repayment	520.00
Total monthly bills	2147.85
Total monthly bills during the winter	2392.85
Net	537.33
Net in winter	292.33

(The house is All Electric with electric radiators for heat)

Try feeding a family of 4 with 2 growing kids, and a cat. Buy groceries, clothes, household supplies like toilet paper and soap. There is nothing left to go anywhere or do anything. No movies, no eating out. No real ability to save for a rainy day or major car repair/replacement.

The thing that hurts me the most is the ability or lack of it to go on vacations. If it weren't for a tax return we couldn't even do that. I get 10 days a year for vacation but our tax return only allows us to be able to afford about 5 days somewhere, the rest of the vacation time left has to be taken at home. At this point I wonder how many people reading this are sitting at home thinking I thought it was only me!

(During the writing of this book I brought up the subject again with my employer and was laid off the next day, nice huh?).

I know right now that many people would say make your wife work, then you would have money for extra things. And I say yeah and have a stranger raise our 2 year old. Any money my wife would make would pay someone to watch our son. So where is the point in that? I could see if I made a low wage and the wife had to work, but why should she? I make $48,000 a year most people would love to have that much money, but it gets eaten up anyway.

When I was a kid a working adult could afford a small apartment on just a minimum wage job. This is not true today. A young adult leaves home but has to have roommates to have a half way decent place to live. Most couples start out; have a kid or 2 and are stuck working their lives away, to not make it in the end. How many kids have kids of their own and have to move back in with their parents?

If they do move out on their own, they can barely afford to live in the worst, poorest neighborhoods. What do you get when you have to pay someone else to raise your kids while you work? What happens when your kids grow up in a bad neighborhood because that is all you can afford? You get good kids that grow into bad adults!

Most parenting experts would say it is the parents who are to blame if their kids go bad. This is only partially true. Parents that are completely consumed on a daily basis with just trying to pay the rent and provide food for their families are going to have kids that no matter what they try to do to prevent it, their kids are going to grow into bad adults.

Chapter 9

Do your Best

Try and feed your family well. Forget that, not only is what you can afford not going to be healthy, as most of the least expensive foods are the least healthy to eat. The less expensive the food the more likely it is to be carbohydrates and feeding people mostly carbohydrates leads to fat kids. Parents tend to stay slimmer because they go to work, sometimes at more than one job and they eat much less.

Take milk for example. A few months ago they announced that due to high gas prices the price of milk was going up. Where does that fit into the price of milk? At the current price of gas it doesn't cost the price of milk to go up 40 cents a gallon, but that is what they tell you and do to the price. If the price of gas is up, that is a fixed cost that is offset by a tax break for the truck that delivers the milk. So the price of gas is up which would reflect a 1-2 cent adjustment in the price of milk, NOT 40 cents.

There is a shuffle here as well, if you remember the rule of supply and demand that I talked about earlier, well what happens is the dairy board gets a government subsidy and pays the milk farmers to pour some of its milk projection down the drain. So instead of paying the 85 cents that a gallon of milk should be costing you, you pay $3.00 a gallon. Get the picture? The government is actively involved in raising the prices in the diary, meat and produce markets.

Cheese is the one that gets me, it takes milk, some enzymes and a little churning to make cheese, yet it is one of the most expensive things in the store. It takes a tub filled with milk, the enzymes, you churn it for a day or so then let it sit for another day and then you cut it up and package it. That is it, 35 cents worth of milk and enzymes to make a pound of cheese. This sells for $6.00 or more per pound. I could go on forever about food, but one thing I will say is that food in the stores is essentially bad for your health. Everything is processed to death so that it has little or no nutritional value. Then they add all kinds of chemicals to it, so it doesn't lose its color or rot before you buy it.

When The Kellogg brothers invented corn flakes it was made to last for 2 weeks. Now packaged foods stay on shelves for weeks and months at a time, without going bad. The government and the corporations will tell you this is to protect you, but how is food still good for you after sitting so long. This is how they make money. They are not constantly making more cereal to replace the boxes we eat. 2 or 3 times a year they make the cereal and send it out to the stores where it sits until it is gone and then more is ordered every 3 months or so. The only ones benefiting here are the corporations that make it and sell it to you, it is not healthy.

If you think I am wrong, go out and pick an apple off a tree, put it on a saucer and leave it on the kitchen table. How long does it take to go bad? About a week and that was fresh picked. But the common practice in the grocery business is for fruits and vegetables to be picked 2 weeks before they are even ripe, so that by the time they get to your table, they have not gone bad. The food has not ripened on the tree or vine and is immature in not only its size and color; its nutritional value is much less than it should be.

Take another fresh picked apple from your tree and one of the exact same kind from any major grocery store, compare them and then taste the fresh one first, and then the store bought one. YOU will see and taste a difference. This is the kind of crap they make us pay for when they should be paying us. If people are not properly nourished, they will be less healthy and prone to illness; sick people are easier to control.

This is the fourth factor in the Erosion of Freedom.

All packaged and processed foods are loaded with chemicals, preservatives and a special ingredient called MSG, or Monosodium Glutamate. MSG is produced naturally in the brain, but as an additive it can be deadly. Too much of it can kill you. Unfortunately it is in everything, including fast food. The food industry uses MSG to enhance the flavor and taste of their foods. As an additive it is 10 times stronger than salt, and most people know how bad salt can be for you. Ever have a bowl of homemade soup? It may need a pinch of salt, but soup companies add MSG constantly. If regular salt is bad for you when you use too much imagine how bad MSG is for you. MSG should be banned in the US.

Recently state governments have made laws requiring that trans-fats be removed from everything. Trans-fats are known to contribute to heart disease, specifically in clogging the arteries of the heart. This is a good thing, BUT, more people die from stroke each year and the one thing that would benefit us all greatly would be to ban MSG, that hasn't happened.

As long as I am talking about food, nutrition and health, I can't go on down the road without talking about cigarettes. Natural tobacco is not altogether unhealthy. The Native Americans grew and cultivated tobacco for centuries without being unhealthy from smoking it. Tobacco is produce and produce rots after a week or so, so the tobacco industry pumps it full of chemicals and preservatives to keep it from rotting and making it more addictive. As a commercial product tobacco is very bad, you can't smoke it indoors anywhere anymore, except Las Vegas, but why do they tell us it is so very bad and yet they do not ban it too? In the early 70s cigarette advertising was removed from TV, this was a concession that appeased the anti-tobacco people, to actually shut them up and still allow the tobacco industry to continue to operate. Well heck, tobacco is one of the biggest industries in this country; some of the major brands are sold globally. The tobacco industry spends millions and millions on Washington Law makers, so of course tobacco is still sold everywhere.

Chapter 10

Health Care Of Course!

Corp. Greed at its finest!

Back in 1999-2000 I used to watch the Chris Rock show on HBO. I love smart comedy and Chris is one smart guy and funny too! In his stand up show, he talked about health care and he asked one important question, "When was the last time Medicine cured anything?" The answer to that is Polio. At one time it had been a billion dollar industry and was wiped out of existence overnight when the cure was found. Before the cure hospitals had whole floors where they took care of the polio patients; companies made a fortune manufacturing those iron lung machines. The polio patients had to stay in the hospital and in the iron lung machines for weeks or months.

Look at AIDS, people are no longer dying quickly from AIDS. They have medicine that will keep them alive for years now, it doesn't cure the AIDS, but you can live with it,

As Chris Rock said they manage the disease now. "There is no money in curing it, but managing it with drugs is big money and profits." Why come up with a cure that is a few pills when they can keep you buying their drugs for 20-30 years, why should they care if your quality of life is poor, at least in their minds you are alive! Why sell you a cure for $20 when they can get 10 of thousands of dollars for keeping you alive with the disease? Who doesn't see the evil in this?

Several years back, in 2003 or 2004, I watched a primetime news show about a little girl who had some kind of cancer that was growing on her spine. Her doctor gave her an injection of a new medicine and it cured the little girl in just a few days. Her cancer was completely gone. So when the doctor reported this to the pharmaceutical company, what did they do? They pulled the medicine saying that they would not be able to market it! Even the doctor was taken aback by this. A cure for a cancer, was not marketable? What crap! Just thinking about this and all those innocent kids dying rather than giving them the cure, makes me absolutely nauseous! What they were really saying is, don't sell a cure for a few hundred dollars when we can make tens of thousands for chemo and radiation therapies. And then if they survive we can make ten of thousands more helping them to recover from the harsh effects of the chemo and radiation.

The cures are out there, most people will agree with this. But how do we get them? That is the 500 billion dollar question, after all that is the amount of profits to be lost in curing one disease. Stem cell and T-cell research look very hopeful in treating things where damage has occurred as with a heart attack. The research shows that T-cell infusions can assist in the re-growth of the tissues damaged by the heart attack. So of course President Bush outlawed this kind of research. Look at how commonly clear this is, something is a strong candidate to heal or cure something, so off a medical research or pharmaceutical company official goes to the White House with a check. *"Mr. President we want you to have this private donation of nearly a million dollars please sign this law and we will give you the money"*.

Chapter 11

Housing

Remember back in my opening I used the expression that in America, 1% of the population of the US owns and controls 85% of it.

This means that 99% percent of the Population controls/owns 15%, and of these 99%, less than 50% own their own homes.

Housing is another big one in my book. The prices of homes have soared and in some circumstances to much more than 1000%! With the rise in home prices comes the rise in property taxes, the thought process being if you can afford the higher price of the house you can afford the higher taxes. For the last 10 years, I have found that to buy a new home takes two incomes; this is for the 99% of the population. There is an economic rule that is useful here. This rule is a guide line for budgeting your monthly income effectively, it is all but dead today, here's why.

A mortgage or rental payment should be 25% of your NET monthly income, so if you clear $4000 a month you can afford to pay $1000 for a mortgage or for rent. Applying this rule quickly shows that mortgage and rentals payments are often way above what they should be. WAY ABOVE. How many people do you know that pay far more then this for housing, just about everybody; I know.

When I was a kid my single mother rented us a 2 bedroom 1 bath house for $90 a month in a good neighborhood back in 1968. When my mother finally moved out in 1979, 11 years later the rent was $750 a month. This was more than an 800 % rise in rent. Here is another rule I came up with on renting a house, so that you find something affordable. Look at the rent versus square footage on the basis of less than a dollar per square foot, so if a house is 1000 sq. feet the rent should be less than $1000. The rule as I apply it works out to $1 per 1.5 sq. feet so a 1500 sq. foot house would rent for $1000!

The problem with that sq. footage rule is that people that own rental properties have one thing in mind and that is to make as much money as they can. Most people who own a house that they rent out should be content with having the renters pay their equity in it, after all, that is supposed to be the principle reason for owning rental property. After renting out the house for 20 or 30 years, they sell it and pocket a nice little nest egg for their retirement or leave it as an inheritance. Nowadays they buy a house with a ridiculous mortgage rate and pass that onto their renters in high rental rates. This does not make good renters, they will only stay long enough to get or afford something better. So owners try to get high move in deposits and charge higher rents, this creates a never ending cycle of constantly rising prices!

Mortgages are too easy to get, after all you can't run off with the house it's stuck to the ground. Mortgage companies have flooded the markets with easy to get loans and people who want rental properties snatch them up like frogs sitting on a log catching flies. The rates are so insane that the people buying rental properties have to try to charge high rents in bad neighborhoods, and because they are not content to make equity and think that they must make cash back every month the only people that will rent from them are the ones that move in and stop paying rent and then you have to go to court and it takes 90 days to evict them. That's 90 days with no money coming in for the house or apartment.

In Sept. 2007 French banks froze the assets of 3 US funding groups that sold mortgages globally; these 3 groups sold the kind of mortgages that were too easy to get, no qualifying. This move by the French banks caused temporary mortgage crisis, in the US.

The problem with these easy to get mortgages is because people are getting mortgages on property that they can't afford, they take these mortgages in the hope of turning around and selling the property for a higher price in less than 30 days, if the house doesn't sell, the banks foreclose! Oct 2007 shows record high foreclosures in the US. The underlying problem is the people getting these types of mortgages are from the "middle class" in their attempt to get ahead of the flood of high prices.

Another big housing scam is requiring a credit check to rent a house or an apartment, they typically want to charge $35-$50 per each adult to rent you a house or apartment, there are 2 reasons for this; first a credit check costs them $3-$5, so 2 adults just netted them a profit of

$60-$90. Some of the more desirable apartment complexes will have 1 apartment available but will collect 200 credit applications per week at $50 each times 2 adults earning them a whopping $20,000. Some places will keep 1 or 2 apartments empty on purpose just so they can keep that kind of cash coming in. WHAT A SCAM! Many of these management companies will do this without the owner(s) even knowing about it and collecting a fee from the owner(s) for their services. I say that if you have a job and they can verify your income is sufficient to pay your rent that should be it! Even if you have perfect credit they will tell you that you credit isn't good enough so that they can charge you a much higher deposit to move in. So you move out, you leave the place clean, you painted it and there is not a single stain on the carpet. Yet you try to get your $1000 cleaning deposit back and get $100, according to them the place was so dirty it needed $500 worth of cleaning and it needed brand new paint. People get away with this sort of thing everywhere!

A few months ago we went to look at a house to buy; we had to meet the realtor at her office so that she could go with us to show us the house. The place was a few hours from our current house, so we packed the kids in the car on a Saturday and off we went. When we got there I went into see the realtor, I told her I had called her about the house and was there at the appointed time to go see the house. The realtor informed me that if I wanted to see the house I had to pay for a credit check before she would take us to the house. We wanted to see the house, if we didn't like it for some reason why would we consider buying it, pay $100 to see a house that we might not like! Screw you!

I absolutely cannot talk about housing without commenting on New Orleans and the

Katrina Disaster. Kanye West, the Hip Hop Artist was right when he said, "Bush Doesn't like Black People". When Bush was elected Governor of Texas and was informed that the blacks did not vote in large percentages for him, he stated "They won't get any help from me" As I stated earlier, Bush the knot headed idiot can't keep his rich spoiled mouth shut. You run for public life to help do things for the people that elected you, but as is true throughout America, most politicians run to help themselves to a huge slice of the corporations' profit pie.

After Katrina the US did not move quickly and effectively to help those in New Orleans, too many people died simply for lack of drinking water! Only those in the affected areas who had insurance have been able to put their lives back together. The poor areas have not been rebuilt! Bush has a war to pay for; he was not going to spend the money on the good citizens who needed it! Most of the people left homeless have been moved out and will never be able to return.

What I see happening in New Orleans' damaged areas is that they will sit until the property owners loose their rights to them, some large developer will come in and buy up all the land really cheap and build expensive homes on it. The levees will be rebuilt and no hurricane will be able to knock them down. The levees that were there before were substandard, but that was the plan all along. Levee technology in places like Holland far exceeds that that was in place in New Orleans.

I recently saw a scientific report where a weatherman claims to have manipulated Hurricane Katrina to turn north and smash into the New Orleans area. The reason he states was to prevent Katrina from running its course along the US gulf coast, and smashing into the hundreds of oil drilling rigs. Save the oil kill the people!

Chapter 12

A Scam Played on Me

Here is my favorite scam; this is my real electric bill! My utility company is NYSEG, New York State Electric and Gas (The name alone sounds like it should be a government regulated Utility, but it is not)

The first part shows the meter reading for the month, and then they list the various charges.

Basic service charge	15.40
Bill issuance charge	0.89
On-peak delivery charge	29.44
Off-peak delivery charge	3.08
Transition charge	-0.07
SBC\RPS charge	1.90
Delivery Sub Total	50.64

This is only what they charge to get the electricity to me, there are no electricity charges listed above; I have not gotten that far yet.

A basic service charge, this is a membership fee. Then they charge a fee to make this bill!

Then 2 charges per the kilowatts used, TO deliver the electricity to my house.

I am being charged just for being their customer to the total of 50.64!

Now the actual electricity charges for the amount we used.

On-peak Supply charge	62.93
Off-peak Supply charge	9.63
Merchant function charge	2.80
Electricity Sub Total	75.36

A total electric bill of $126.00.

This is based on exactly 1000 kilowatt hours used for the month. Interesting how the amount used and the total bill are in nice round numbers. My friend said to change this otherwise it looks suspiciously made up, I swear to you it is not and I have kept a copy of the bill I used to enter this data, just in case someone wants me to prove it!

The 75.36 is a fair amount for the electricity we do use, but all those other charges just to have their service is a total sham. In many parts of New York, you do not get billed for the delivery charges, only the electricity used by you. In New York City, they pay for only the amount they use. So here is the scam. In New York City there is only one provider, Con-Ed. Here in Upstate New York there are several companies you can buy your electricity from, but it all still comes from NYSEG. They own the lines and relay stations, but because you can buy electricity from one of 3 other companies, you have to pay absurd delivery charges. Even though I am loyal to NYSEG, I still get charged all the extra "goodies". Understand that delivery charges do not mean that a truck comes to my house and brings electricity, what it means is that they charge me a fee to send the electricity to my house over their own lines and relay stations. This means that electricity in New York City is regulated but not upstate New York!

Chapter 13

I'll Take Cremation for 800, Alex

I'll take Cremation for 800, Alex

Here is another crazy business that simply takes advantage of people at a bad time in their life and that is when a loved one has passed away. In the old days, when a person died or was killed, the family cleaned up the body, dressed it in its nicest clothes, laid it out on the dining room table, for all the friends and neighbors to come by and visit and the next day they put the body in a box, if they had one, if not they just buried it in the churchyard or the backyard. It did not cost Money!

Nowadays it costs at the minimum $6000.00; when you die everyone has their hand open to take your money. If you die in the hospital, the funeral home will not come over and take your body, unless someone pays them first, a minimum of $2000.00, then you buy a casket, arrange for a burial place, have a service, all of this costs money. If you have insurance they get even slicker. The counselor at the funeral will tell you "don't worry about a thing, we will bill the insurance company for you, you don't have to do anything". But what they do is charge everything and anything to the insurance company.

Since you have insurance, everything you have picked out costs double, they don't tell you that, but they bill it that way. You picked out the $2000 casket in gray, but since they are going to bill the insurance, they switch your choice for the $6000 casket, also in gray. It looks exactly the same but it will last in the ground 3 times as long.

I mean come on they set out chairs at the grave site for people to sit on. A dozen or two dozen chairs, they will bill for two dozen even if they only put out one dozen, and bill your insurance $200 per chair. You are not buying the chairs, they have their own or they may rent them, but they charge you a fee to take them over there, another fee to set them up and another fee to bring them back, plus the $200 for each chair. You had insurance for $30,000 and you figure after what was supposed to be a $6000 funeral you would receive $24,000 to help ease your pain, but the funeral was billed as a $16,875 funeral, leaving you $13,125.

Now imagine if you had a mortgage to pay still, or some leftover hospital bills, you end up wiped out, you have to sell the house where you lived for 35 years and you have no savings left. This is insane, but it happens all the time and to a lot of people. It's just another grand rip off.

Chapter 14

The Others

Fast cars and faster profits

When I was a teenager in the 70s, people were buying new cars for around $3500. Now what is the price of a new car, the average is $35,000! Again we see prices rise at 10 times or 1000%; just like gas prices. Oil companies and car makers top the list of richest, largest corporations in the world, imagine that! 30 years ago if you took care of that car it would last and last, now even if you take super good care of it, you will be lucky to get 100,000 miles out of it without a major repair expense.

Most new cars will have to have a transmission or engine replaced at 80,000 miles. Cars today are made to last 6-7 years, just long enough for you to pay off your loan on it, and then you have to go out and buy a new one and start all over again, this goes not only for the auto makers, but finance companies, auto repair shops and so on. They don't want that new car to last any longer, because if they did they wouldn't sell as many and make so many billions in profit for their stock holders.

The Postal Scam

You will be surprised at this or maybe not, but to my way of thinking this is an outrage. What is the price of a first class stamp, today it is 41 cents. Any letter you send up to one ounce will cost you 41 cents. But did you know that large corporations don't pay nearly this much, in fact less than half. Today I got a letter, 2 pages long in a number 10 envelope from my bank about some new offer for insurance for bank account members. A number 10 envelope is the standard business size. The bank paid postage of just 19 cents! I know you are thinking well they get bulk rates, and of course the answer is yes, but when was the last time you got bulk rates?

Never! You buy a book of stamps, which is 20-41 cent stamps, that is buying in bulk but are you getting a bulk discount, of course not.

As I have said everywhere in this book everyone is out to take your money. The difference here is the US government is doing it to you. A large corporation can afford to pay full postage far more easily than you, yet they are the ones getting the huge break in the price. It is not like they can use another postal company to send their letters, so why do these multi-billion dollar corporations get such huge breaks in the cost of their postage? It's the law. As I said in the opening of this book, corporations rule the US, giving donations and trips and vacations, so that the law makers will vote for laws that benefit the corporations and leave you high and dry.

The Dentist

Last year I went to the dentist, I knew I had a cavity that needed filling. It never hurt but since I had dental insurance I figured why wait until it becomes a tooth ache. The dentist gave me x-rays and then I sat in his chair so he could look at my teeth. He looked in my mouth and then wrote down some stuff on my chart never once saying a word to me. Then I was lead out, I thought I was going to get my tooth filled, BIG SURPRISE!

In the front office I met with the receptionist, she told me that they checked my insurance. She told me that if I wanted my tooth filled I needed to pay $660.00 which was my 30% share of the 70-30 insurance that I had. She told me that I needed a root canal, a crown and of course a good cleaning. A total of $2200.00 to be paid by me and the insurance company. At this point I figured that they were trying to stick it to me and the insurance company. And I was right. I had looked at the x-ray while in the chair and I saw that the cavity did not go below the gum line, so it was not into the root. So I walked out telling them that I would think about it.

I called my friend to get the address of his dentist. I went right over, I talked to the dentist first, I told him about the other place. He took just one x-ray and filled the tooth and cleaned my teeth for a cost to me of $45.00. No root canal, No crown. The tooth has not bothered me at all and never got worse as the first dentist office had said it would if I didn't get the root canal.

Although this is one dentist this is a classic example of how everyone tries to get a bigger piece of the money pie, in this specific case, this guy was out to get it from me and the insurance company.

Chapter 15

Countdown to Revolution

Back to a reflection of President Bush for a moment; after taking office he took a large donation from the Health Insurance Industry to revamp Medicare. (See the movie Sicko for more on this). The purpose of revamping Medicare was that the additional parts of Medicare require joining a private health insurance company to get your prescriptions. Now seniors have co-payments up to $2000.00 per year for their prescriptions. Seniors can not and should not have to pay these ridiculous sums. This law was enacted with just one purpose, to give the private Health Insurance companies HIGHER PROFITS.

People all over this country cannot afford to pay the high rates that are required for health insurance coverage. With all the taking of their money going on, they just do not have enough left to pay these kind of high rates even if they were lowered significantly. These Health

Insurance companies are never going to lower the rates enough for people to afford.

The purpose of my writing this book is twofold; I have talked about the ways that the US government and corporations have knowingly united to take everything you make through higher prices. This is just one of the factors in the Erosion of Freedom Doctrine. I have discussed all four factors in this book. All of the factors together create a state that is ripe for take over by tyrannical forces.

Remember that back in the 1700s the US was persecuted by England's King George with high taxes and the fixing of high prices. This persecution angered us enough to revolt, fight a long war were 1000s of lives were lost, just for the ability to rule ourselves, by Democracy. Democracy has been killed off in this country with greedy politicians and even greedier corporations kicking dirt on its open grave. The people, the 297 million Americans who are not millionaires, are not to blame. They have been lied to and lead into thinking that all is well and due to outside forces, this is as far from the truth as it gets. We have elected people to do our bidding, but those we have elected only do the bidding of the corporations. The corporations are owned by the super wealthy through stock ownership.

It has been a busy year in the fortune-hunting business. Strong equity markets combined with rising real estate values and commodity prices pushed up fortunes from Mumbai to Madrid. Forbes pinned down 946 billionaires, including 178 newcomers and 17 people who climbed back into the ranks after being absent for a year or more. Two-thirds of last year's billionaires are richer. Only 17% are poorer, including 32 who fell below the billion-

dollar mark. The billionaires' combined net worth climbed by $900 billion to $3.5 trillion. That equates to $3.6 billion apiece

From Forbes.com Dated April 27, 2007

In the article above look at the second sentence, 'Strong equity markets combined with rising real estate values and commodity prices pushed up fortunes'. 'Strong Equity Markets' refers to the shares these people own in companies. 'Real estate values' are the soaring prices on housing and other real property like land and buildings. Commodity prices are Oil, Corn Wheat, Diary and Meat. Get the point? These people manipulate higher prices which results in their billions growing into more billions for them! The government does not make or print more money so this money can only come from one place and that is from, you and I.

And so the rich get richer while 'The People' strive to make a living getting by paycheck to paycheck. Any person who can't afford basic things like health care insurance has lost their freedom. I do not seek to destroy the rich and take all their money to give to The People; I am not Robin Hood anew. I seek to stop their continued growth of wealth at OUR expense.

Years ago when Barbara Walters interviewed Bill Gates, he commented on his wealth by saying this, "After the first few billion, you can not live better, eat better or travel better, so the rest is just not important" If it is not important why do these people continue to horde it for themselves? If a billion dollars of worth is the threshold, why keep the rest of it? There are millions in this country who could use a share of it. Use it to give people jobs instead of sending those jobs to foreign countries. Or buy needy families health care? There are hundreds of things that they can use this money for that would benefit The People. Of course they could not help everyone that is just not practical, but they are not going to help anyone.

Now for the final harsh reality. I have said all throughout this book that 3 million Americans are worth at least one million dollars. 3 million Americans is 1% of the US population or 1 in every 1 hundred Americans. According to the US government only one out of every 1200 American is a millionaire. That means that it is not 3 million Americans, but 250,000! That is 1/12 of what you have read about here, it is not 1 % but 0.0833%. Hence there are not 297 Million Americans, but 299,750,000 who are poor!

The media reports it as 1% of the US Population, but the more accurate records of the government show that it is 12 times worse than what you have read in this book, if reading about 3 million Americans made you angry or upset, then finding out that only 250,000 millionaire Americans should surely make you want to do something to affect change.

The US is number one in wealth for the 250,000 Americans that have it, but that is about all that the US leads the world in. We are not number one in Education, Health care, or care for the poor and homeless. We should set the example in all of these areas. In Sicko, Michael Moore shows that people in England live longer than we do, because of its health care system, this is only partly true. In England the farmers bring fresh Meat, Produce, and dairy to the town markets, they live longer because they eat healthier, and they have better health care.

It appears that I blame all things on the Republican presidents, while this is true because they have done the most damage I want to point out, that Democratic presidents have also made mistakes, it is after all a situation of trial and error. It seems as President, one would want to look at what worked in the past and what did not and implement those policies that worked the best. Unfortunately, they do not take this approach to the office at all. Politicians are such narcissistic creatures that their own egos will not allow them to do anything or repeat a policy that worked in the past. Being so narcissistic, they enter office with a huge bag of favors that have been bought and paid for by the corporations. They blindly set out to resolve all the favors without much thought to the Real Americans out there who work and toll for the benefit of the few elite members of the 'super class'.

Hence,

- From this day forward The People of the United States of America, will no longer allow out of control pricing.

- We will not work our lives away so that the super rich few can become richer!

- It MUST be made illegal for anyone running for public office to take donations, trips and travel from the Corporations.

- We will through legal process, remove those elected officials that take donations, trips and travel in exchange for favors for the Corporations.

- Any elected official that takes an office and does not do the bidding of those that elected him or her will be removed.

- A ceiling cap of not more than 25% above costs for all goods and services sold in the US is a must. This is 25 cents per dollar that is to be the maximum profit margin.

- Dependence on oil, both foreign and domestic must be eliminated within 10 years if not sooner. This is the Mark of a True American Law Maker or Leader

- We will strive to elect only those worthy of the Mark of a True American Law Maker or Leader.

- 1 Adult member of every family MUST join in this fight to take back our country. That Adult must register to vote, in this way we can ensure that we as a whole affect change.

- Church groups, parent association groups, veterans groups and all civic groups in every town and city will gather together to find the best candidate that will fulfill the above mentioned obligations to their office.

- To achieve these goals we will use NO forms of force OR violence, EVER. By showing them that our resolve and will are greater than theirs shall we succeed.

These are the terms of the Second American Revolution and they are not open for debate or negotiation. If we allow any form of negotiation on this issues we have lost, therefore our resolve is finite. By creating a second revolution we strip away the power of the wealthy to buy candidates and favors of the elected law makers. By stripping away their power we restore Democracy to its rightful place in our government, never allowing a situation where Democracy is under attack and with a knife to its throat.

Only by working together as one united group will this be accomplished. Waiting for others to do this for you will not suffice. In as much as you all are victims of the Erosion of Freedom; you must ALL unite to affect change.

I have long thought to write and be a writer. I did not want to write stories of fiction or magical places, I leave that to those who are gifted in such writings. I told myself years ago I would not write until I gained a passion for a subject. In the years of watching my own family and loved ones struggle with money, or hearing a friend or stranger complain about the way things are and then concluding to themselves that nothing could be done to change it, I have become passionate about saving this country.

I am not narcissistic enough to want to run for any office or take over the seat of government. I am simply the messenger that brings the message. I am but a patriot, the person that brings the news that Democracy can be resurrected and brought back to its glory. I am not a prophet or chosen one, I have seen the evil and I wish to open your eyes to it. History has showed us that all the great governments and empires failed and died because they did not take care of their people. I will not let American Democracy go down without a fight. Unite now, in saving your money and your financial well being for yourself and your family's benefit, you restore TRUE justice and Democracy to America.

"When you see a rattlesnake poised to strike, you do not wait until he has struck before you crush him."
Franklin D. Roosevelt

"These are the times that try men's souls. The summer soldier and the sunshine patriot will, in this crisis, shrink from the service of their country; but he that stands it now, deserves the love and thanks of man and woman."
Thomas Paine, American Patriot

"We are the standard-bearers in the only really authentic revolution, the democratic revolution against tyrannies. Our strength is not to be measured by our military capacity alone, by our industry, or by our technology. We will be

remembered, not for the power of our weapons, but for the power of our compassion, our dedication to human welfare."

Hubert Humphrey

There is one last piece of business that we must take care of. The Bush Administration has not only created a society in the US of profit takers, including himself and his family, but he took the US into a completely false war using lies and deception to accomplish the goals of the Iraq Club. This alone would make him a War Criminal, but he took it even further, by ordering the US military to use DU (Depleted Uranium) on Iraq Targets.

DU is the left over Uranium from a nuclear reactor after it is no longer usable for electricity production. It is still radioactive for 1000s of years. Normally it is sealed in containers and buried somewhere. It is not usable to make any kind of nuclear bomb, but can be ground into a powder and used to coat large caliber bullets. These bullets were used in Iraq and fired at their tanks and other military vehicles to make the radioactive. The Iraqi country side is littered with radioactive military vehicles.

Besides the economic reforms that I have talked about and I advocate for, some form of punishment is required for George Bush and His Administration. I suggest prison! Anyone in His Administration, who had prior knowledge of the use of DU before it was sent to Iraq, should be tried and put in prison.

www.ingramcontent.com/pod-product-compliance
Lightning Source LLC
Chambersburg PA
CBHW060631290526
45793CB00001B/209